www.megalithicmonumentsofireland.com

POCKET GUIDE SERIES

OTHER TITLES BY THIS AUTHOR

STONES OF TIME
THE PREHISTORIC TEMPLES & TOMBS OF IRELAND
Copyright © **Dec. 2010**

DOLMENS OF SOUTH EAST IRELAND
Portal Tombs of
Carlow - Dublin - Kilkenny - Waterford
Wexford and Wicklow
Copyright © **Feb. 2011**

www.megalithicmonumentsofireland.com

POCKET GUIDE SERIES

A POCKET GUIDE TO
MEGALITHIC MONUMENTS IN CLARE

VOLUME XIV

PHILIP I. POWELL

MEGAS LITHOS PRESS

DUBLIN, IRELAND

Copyright © **Mar.2011 M M I**
www.megalithicmoumentsofireland.com
All rights reserved.

ISBN -13: 978-1460998885
ISBN-10: 146099888X

Printed in the U.S.A.

www.megalithicmonumentsofireland.com

POCKET GUIDE SERIES

www.megalithicmonumentsofireland.com

POCKET GUIDE SERIES

ACKNOWLEDGEMENTS

Borlase, W.C. *The Dolmens of Ireland.* London, Chapman & Hall, 1897.

Cooney, G. *Neolithic Landscapes of Ireland.* London. Routledge. 2000.

Harbison, P.
1939- ; b. Dublin, ed. Glenstal, UCD; archaeologist; *Axes, Daggers, and Halberds of the Early Bronze Age in Ireland (1969); The Archaeology of Ireland* (Bodley Head 1976); *Pre-Christian Ireland from the First Settlers to the Early Celts* (Guild 1988)

Jackson, K.H. *A Window on the Iron Age.* 1964.

MacAlister, R. A. S. *Corpus Inscriptionum Insularum Celticarum* (2 volumes. Dublin, 1946–9)

O'Kelly, C. *Illustrated Guide to New Grange and the other Boyne Monuments.* Cork. C O'Kelly 1978.

O'Kelly, M.J Early Ireland: *An Introduction to Irish Prehistory.* Cambridge. Cambridge University Press. 1988.

www.megalithicmonumentsofireland.com

POCKET GUIDE SERIES

O'Rahilly, T.F. 1946 *Early Irish History and Mythology.*

Shee Twohig, E. *Irish Megalithic Tombs*, Shire Archaeology 1990. - *The Megalithic Art of Western Europe.* Oxford, Clarendon Press.1981.

De Valera, R. O'Nualllain, S. 1972. *Survey of Megalithic Tombs of Ireland, Volumes I, II, III, IV.* Dublin. Stationery Office.

Ziegler, Sabine. *Die Sprache der altirischen Ogam-Inschriften* (Göttingen, 1994)

Powell, P. *Stones Of Times.* 2010. *Dolmens Of South East Ireland.* 2011.

Powell, P. *Photographs and Illustrations.*

National Museum of Ireland, Dublin

Caherconnell Stone Fort Visitor Center

The Craggaunowen Project

www.megalithicmonumentsofireland.com

POCKET GUIDE SERIES

CONTENTS

I	**Introduction**	**9**
II	**Megalithic Tombs**	**14**
	Portal Tombs	**16**
	Wedge Tombs	**22**
	Other Tombs	**46**
III	**Stone Rows & Stone Pairs**	**53**
IV	**Standing Stones**	**59**
V	**Ogham Stones**	**91**
VI	**Bullaun Stones**	**95**
VII	**Other Sites**	**99**
VIII	**Glossary**	**106**
IX	**Index of Images**	**115**
X	**Special Notes**	**117**

www.megalithicmonumentsofireland.com

POCKET GUIDE SERIES

www.megalithicmonumentsofireland.com

INTRODUCTION

The introduction of farming into Ireland led to a monumental change in society on the island as human beings had begun to take the first steps in controlling their own environment. They cleared the uplands of their trees and removed the boulders and stones left over from the Ice age. At first it was a simple method of growing crops in small clearings for making course bread. The domestication of wild animals began with the holding of these animals in pens for their milk, meat and pelts, freeing them from the daily pursuit of game and gathering of plants and berries. This was an enormous change to these early farmers, as they were not now reliant on the seasons for their supply of food and with gradual improvements in crop growing, they were able to store excess foods for lean periods of time.

The Mesolithic life style of the hunter-gatherer did not end immediately but was gradually replaced by the more settled life style of farming and with it the beginnings of communities and ownership of the land.

The 3rd period of the Stone Age, the Neolithic Age, or New Stone Age, had begun and with it the dawn of a new age that would totally transform the world and human society and its consequences are still felt to this day in the way we feed ourselves and the type of communal society we live in.

Exactly when and from where this new way of life appeared in Ireland we cannot be certain of but it is safe to say it happened around 4,500 BC the transitional period between the Mesolithic and Neolithic Age. The transformation was gradual and took many centuries to spread throughout the island.

Archaeologists have long debated where the influences of megalithic tomb building had come, and at first pointed to the Mediterranean region but radio carbon dating evidence shows that tomb building was taking place some two thousand years before the pyramids in Egypt and most likely evolved independently along the Atlantic coastline between communities from present day France, Britain and northern Spain and in isolation from eastern Europe. The meaning and function of these megalithic monuments still puzzles archaeologists to this day and only recently have we begun to understand their construction and complexity and shed some light on what religious rituals they may have enacted as part of their burial rites. The tradition of megalithic tomb building lasted in Europe until the end of the stone age around 2,500 BC but in Ireland it continued on well into the Bronze Age, as late as 1,700 BC, with some tombs in the south west being used even later, around 1,200 BC and many tombs continued to be used well into the Iron Age, around 200 BC.

POCKET GUIDE SERIES

www.megalithicmonumentsofireland.com

POCKET GUIDE SERIES

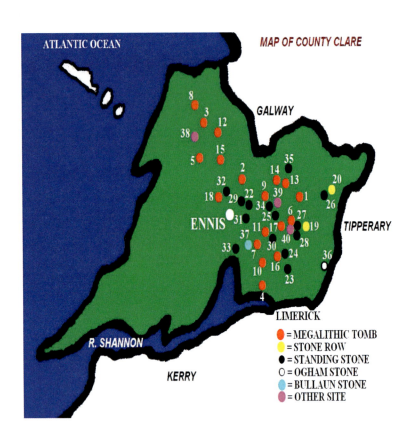

COUNTY CLARE

County Clare, **'Contae an Chláir'**, is located on the west coast of Ireland and is north-west of the River Shannon, the largest river in Ireland and Britain. There has been human activity in the Clare region since the Neolithic period and evidence of this can be seen in the form of ancient dolmens or portal tombs, most famous of these is 'Poulnabrone Dolmen', which translates as 'the hole of sorrows' and is located in an area known as 'The Burren' an area of outstanding natural beauty.

PTOLEMY, the Roman historian, on his map of Ireland in his GEOGRAPHIA dating from 100 AD, identified a tribe known as the 'GANGANI' inhabiting the area around County Clare. During the Early Middle Ages, the area was part of the Kingdom Of Connaught and was ruled by the **Ui Fiachrach Aidhne** until around the 10th century, when it was settled by the **Dalcassians**, the most noted of which was the High King of Ireland, Brian Boru.

MEGALITHIC TOMBS

COURT TOMBS

These types of tombs are generally regarded as being the earliest type of megalithic tomb in Ireland and they consist of a trapezoidal cairn with a typically U-shaped open court, lined by slabs or dry-stone walling, where the entrance leads into the gallery or burial chambers. The court had a ceremonial purpose, with funeral rites being performed before the remains of the dead were placed inside.

PASSAGE TOMBS

These types of tombs, unlike the other tombs, seem to occur in groups or cemeteries and are mainly located in the northern and eastern parts of Ireland. They primarily date from 4,200 BC - 2,900 BC and are instantly recognizable by the large round mound covering the tomb.

PORTAL TOMBS

Portal tombs or **Cromlech** in Irish meaning 'sloping stone', were constructed during the same time-line as court tombs and passage tombs, about 3,800 BC - 2,800 BC. They consist of a rectilinear chamber, usually narrower at the rear, the entrance of which is between two large erect stones called portal stones that are of greater height than the side stones in the chamber. The chamber is covered by a very large, sometimes enormous capstone, the front of which is usually at a very steep angle.

WEDGE TOMBS

Wedge tombs are so called because of their plan and profile and were generally built around 2,500 BC - 2,000 BC, the last phase of the megalithic building in Ireland. They were communal burial tombs with ritual and religious ceremonies being performed at certain times. They consisted of two chambers, one large and one small or ante-chamber and were lined by large erect orthostats which supported one or more capstones.

MEGALITHIC TOMBS (UNCLASSIFIED)

These types of tombs do not conform to the standard features of the other types of tombs and are such termed as unclassified.

BOULDER BURIALS

Boulder Burials are large boulders or capstones of megalithic proportions that rest on a number of smaller supporting stones which usually number 3 or 4 and can often be found with stone circles. They do not form a discernable chamber and they primarily date from the early Bronze Age, 2,400 BC - 500 BC.

CISTS

Cists or Kists consist of a small rectangular stone chest, covered with a stone slab and positioned shallow below the surface. They were for a single grave and date from the late Bronze Age, 1,100 BC.

CLOGHER PORTAL TOMB (1)

This Portal Tomb, not marked on the OS map, is located west of Lough Bridget, north of the Derryruane River on a small, south facing, level platform. The tomb, orientated SW, consists of a very large, rectangular capstone, measuring 4.6m in length, 3.8m in width and 1.8m in depth, two portal stones, one prostrate, two side-stones and a back-stone. The weight of the capstone has pushed the orthostats outwards, resulting in the capstone collapsing into the rectangular chamber. The west portal stone, side-stone and back-stone remain erect and the east portal stone and side-stone have fallen eastwards. The circular mound extends 4m from the structure and cairn material is most evident on the east and north sides.

CO-ORDINATES
52 52' 9.979"N...8 40' 28.441"W

POCKET GUIDE SERIES

CLOGHER PORTAL TOMB

www.megalithicmonumentsofireland.com

POCKET GUIDE SERIES

MOYREE COMMONS PORTAL TOMB (2)

This Portal Tomb, marked on the OS map as **'Dolmen'**, is located east of Ballyteige Lough, **'Loch Bhaile Ui Thaidhg'**, and west of the head waters of the River Castle on a circular mound 10m in diameter. The tomb, orientated east, consists of two erect portal stones, 2.1m in height, two side-stones and a back-stone. The slab like capstone measuring 5.2m in length, has slipped backwards, west, and now rests on the back-stone. The thin, rectangular chamber is 2.8m in length and 1.8m in width and there is some cairn fill present. A large amount of cairn material extends north and west but is less evident at the south and east.

CO-ORDINATES
52 56' 58.053"N...8 56' 56.235"W

POCKET GUIDE SERIES

MOYREE COMMONS PORTAL TOMB

www.megalithicmonumentsofireland.com

POULNABRONE PORTAL TOMB (3)

Poulnabrone Dolmen, **'Poll na mBrón'** meaning 'hole of sorrows', is a portal tomb in the Burren, County Clare, and dates back to the Neolithic period, probably between 4,200-2,900 BC. The tomb consists of a 4m, thin, slab-like, tabular capstone, which is supported by two slender portal stones, which elevate the capstone 1.8m from the ground, creating a chamber, in a 9m long cairn. The cairn helped stabilize the tomb, and would have been much higher originally. The entrance faces north and is crossed by a low sill stone. Excavations found, that between 16 and 22 adults and 6 children were buried under the monument. Items buried with the dead included a polished stone axe, a bone pendant, quartz crystals, weapons and pottery. In the Bronze Age, around 1,700BC, a newborn baby was buried in the portico, just outside the entrance. With its dominating presence on the limestone landscape of the Burren, the tomb was very likely a centre for ceremony and ritual well into the Celtic period. Access is easy, as there is a public car-park and there is an information board on site.

CO-ORDINATES
53 2' 55.264"N...9 8' 24.035"W

POCKET GUIDE SERIES

POULNABRONE PORTAL TOMB

21

www.megalithicmonumentsofireland.com

POCKET GUIDE SERIES

BALLINPHUNTA WEDGE TOMB (4)

This Portal Tomb, marked on the OS map as **'Cromlech'**, is located east of the Owenagarny River, **'Abhalan O' gCearnaigh'**, west of Cratloe, **'An Chreatalach'**, in the modern graveyard of Crughaun Church. The tomb, orientated NE - SW, consists of a large, rectangular capstone, 2.8m in length and 2.3m in width, a single side-stone on the south side and two side-stones on the north side, a back-stone and a door-stone. The south side-stone is supported by two stone buttresses but there are none present on the north side. The chamber, opening to the SW, is 2m in length and 1.8m in width and the whole structure is surrounded by a circular mound 6m in diameter.

CO-ORDINATES
52 42' 12.376"N...8 46' 17.254"W

POCKET GUIDE SERIES

BALLINPHUNTA WEDGE TOMB

www.megalithicmonumentsofireland.com

BALLYGANNER SOUTH WEDGE TOMB (5)

This is probably the biggest Wedge Tomb in the area, marked on the OS map as **'Cromlech'**, and is located in undulating pasture, orientated NE - SW. The chamber is a huge 4.1m in length and 3m in width. The roof-stone, which is broken, is 5m in length, 4m in width and slightly over laps the side-stones. Each of the side-stones is made up of a single huge slab of stone, the full length of the tomb. The ante-chamber in the front of the structure is 1.7m in height and 1.1m in width and has a massive door-slab still in place. The front of the tomb is incorporated into a field wall boundary.

CO-ORDINATES
52 59' 40.88"N...9 9' 42.45"W

POCKET GUIDE SERIES

BALLYGANNER SOUTH WEDGE TOMB

www.megalithicmonumentsofireland.com

DEERPARK NORTH WEDGE TOMB (6)

This fine Wedge Tomb, not marked on the OS map, is located near the summit of a NW facing slope, west of Lough Cullaunyheeda, **'Loch Choileain Ui Shioda'**, and north of the **Craggaunowen Project**. The tomb, orientated NE - SW, consists of two side-stone slabs, 2.1m in length, that support a roof-stone, 1.8m in length. No other stones remain in place, although there are some smaller stones close by that may be connected to the structure.

CO-ORDINATES
52 48' 53.791"N...8 47' 35.226"W

POCKET GUIDE SERIES

DEERPARK NORTH WEDGE TOMB

www.megalithicmonumentsofireland.com

POCKET GUIDE SERIES

FENLOE WEDGE TOMB (7)

This Wedge Tomb, not marked on the OS map, is located in the grounds of Finlough Castle on the northern shores of Finn Lough, **'Fionn Loch'**. The tomb, orientated NE- SW, has been modified with the addition of a roof-stone but the side-stone slabs, 2.5m in length, are in their original positions.

CO-ORDINATES
52 46' 56.209"N...8 50' 2.391"W

POCKET GUIDE SERIES

FENLOE WEDGE TOMB

POCKET GUIDE SERIES

GLENINSHEEN WEDGE TOMB (8)

This fine, small Wedge Tomb, marked on the OS map as **'Cromlech'**, is located on a limestone plateau in the heart of the Burren, north of **Poulnabrone** Portal Tomb. The tomb consists of two side-stone slabs, 2.5m in length, 0.80m in width and 0.35m in depth, a slab-like back-stone, a rectangular roof-stone, 2.6m in length, 2m in width and 0.40m in depth, that rests on the side-stones and back-stone. There is a small orthostat from a possible portico on the south side next to the entrance. The rectangular chamber opens to the SW and there are no visible remains of a mound or cairn.

CO-ORDINATES
52 3' 52.32"N...9 8' 56.53"W

POCKET GUIDE SERIES

GLENINSHEEN WEDGE TOMB

www.megalithicmonumentsofireland.com

POCKET GUIDE SERIES

KILVOYDAN NORTH WEDGE TOMB (9)

This Wedge Tomb, not marked on the OS map, is located west of O'Brien's Big Lough near the summit of N-S ridge, close to a modern driveway. The tomb, orientated NW - SE, has been modified with the addition of a roof-stone and like **Fenloe** wedge tomb, the side-stone slabs are in their original positions. The roof-stone may have been originally part of the structure. No cairn or mound material remains.

CO-ORDINATES
52 53' 13.234"N...8 53' 40.471"W

www.megalithicmonumentsofireland.com

POCKET GUIDE SERIES

KILVOYDAN NORTH WEDGE TOMB

www.megalithicmonumentsofireland.com

KNOCKNALAPPA WEDGE TOMB (10)

This fine Wedge Tomb, marked on the OS map as **'Dermot & Grania's Bed'**, is located near the summit, of a steep NW slope, over-looking Lough Ros Roe, **'Loch an Rois Rua'**, to the NW, with panoramic all round views and east of Newmarket-on-Fergus. The tomb, orientated NW - SE, consists of two large side-stone slabs, a rectangular roof-stone, a back-stone and a blocking stone at the entrance. The roof-stone rests on the two side-stones and back-stone and measures 3.5m in length, 2m in width and 0.90m in depth. The blocking stone is leaning NW and no visible remains of cairn or mounds are present.

CO-ORDINATES
52 46' 15.914"N...8 48' 53.367"W

POCKET GUIDE SERIES

KNOCKNALAPPA WEDGE TOMB

www.megalithicmonumentsofireland.com

POCKET GUIDE SERIES

KNOPOGE WEDGE TOMB (11)

This small Wedge Tomb, marked on the OS map as **'Cromlech'**, is located on good level pasture, east of the standing stones and castle at **Knappogue** and east of Newmarket-on-Fergus. The tomb, orientated NW - SE, consists of four side-stones, two on each side, a back-stone and a roof-stone. The chamber is partially filled with cairn material and the entire structure is sited on a circular mound 10m in diameter.

CO-ORDINATES
52 47' 36.506"N...8 49' 15.231"W

www.megalithicmonumentsofireland.com

POCKET GUIDE SERIES

KNOPOGE WEDGE TOMB

www.megalithicmonumentsofireland.com

MEGGAGH WEDGE TOMB (12)

This small, box-like Wedge Tomb, marked on the Os map as **'Cromlech'**, is located on a south facing slope, in hilly terrain, with panoramic views to the south and west and with limited views east and north. The small chamber is made up from two side-stones and an irregular shaped roof-stone slab, measuring 1.8m in length and 0.80m in width. There is no evidence of cairn or mound present.

CO-ORDINATES
53 2' 5.14"N...9 6' 22.37"W

POCKET GUIDE SERIES

MEGGAGH WEDGE TOMB

39

www.megalithicmonumentsofireland.com

MILLTOWN WEDGE TOMB (13)

This good example of a Wedge Tomb, marked on the OS map as **'Dermot & Grania's Bed'**, is located east of the Tomeen River and east of the town of Ennis, **'Inis'**, in level pasture. The tomb, orientated NNE - SSW, is a box like structure, consisting of two side-stones, 2.5m in length, and a moss covered roof-stone, measuring 2.3m in length. No other stones remain in place and there is no evidence of mound or cairn.

CO-ORDINATES
52 46' 15.914"N...8 48' 53.367"W

POCKET GUIDE SERIES

MILLTOWN WEDGE TOMB

www.megalithicmonumentsofireland.com

NEWGROVE WEDGE TOMB (14)

This Wedge Tomb, marked on the OS map as **'Giant's Grave'**, is located west of the Tomeen River and east of the town of Ennis, **'Inis'**, close to a field boundary ditch. The tomb, orientated NE - SW, consists of two side-stones, a back-stone, a sill-stone and out-walling at the south side. Another erect orthostat, 2m north, may have been part of the outer-walling on the north side. The rectangular roof-stone, split horizontally, measures 2.4m in length and 2.2m in width and is supported by the two side-stones and the back-stone and has caused them to lean slightly SW. Cairn material is evident at the front and back of the tomb, with traces on the north side of the structure.

CO-ORDINATES
52 46' 15.914"N...8 48' 53.367"W

POCKET GUIDE SERIES

NEWGROVE WEDGE TOMB

www.megalithicmonumentsofireland.com

PARKNABINNA WEDGE TOMB (15)

This is most well known of the Wedge Tombs in County Clare, sited as it is very close to the road and is marked on the OS map as **'Cromlech'**. It is very well preserved and is well sited on top of a small hill and is orientated NE - SW. The chamber is 3m in length and 1.8m in width, with two door slabs still in place although one of them is leaning slightly. The roof-stone is 3.2m in length and 2m in width and is covered in grass and soil that maybe the remains of cairn material. The walling, again typical of County Clare, consists of a single slab of stone on either side of the rectangular chamber which is close by a single back-stone. The tomb is easily accessed and is well sign posted from all main roads in the area.

CO-ORDINATES
52 59' 10.77"N...9 5' 45.75"W

POCKET GUIDE SERIES

PARKNABINNA WEDGE TOMB

45

www.megalithicmonumentsofireland.com

POCKET GUIDE SERIES

BALLYSHEEN BEG MEGALITHIC TOMB (16)

This Megalithic Tomb, marked on the OS map as **'Stones'**, is located in the grounds of Walton Lodge Golf Course along with four standing stones. The tomb, orientated NE - SW, consists of three erect orthostats, 0.60m - 0.50m in height, and a small roof-stone. An archaeological survey in the 1960's found no artefacts or human remains on the site.

CO-ORDINATES
52 45' 36.331"N...8 47' 35.871"W

POCKET GUIDE SERIES

BALLYSHEEN BEG MEGALITHIC TOMB

www.megalithicmonumentsofireland.com

DEERPARK MEGALITHIC TOMB (17)

This Megalithic Tomb, not marked on the OS map, is located on a steep south facing slope, in wooded land, north of the car park of **The Craggaunowen Project**. The tomb, with an undefined alignment, consists of a large slab, 2.5m in length, 1.5m in width and 0.65m in depth, which is supported at the east by two small boulders and rests on a small mound at west. The tomb could be the remains of a wedge tomb or possibly be a Boulder Burial.

CO-ORDINATES
52 48' 37.134"N...8 47' 51.024"W

POCKET GUIDE SERIES

DEERPARK MEGALITHIC TOMB

www.megalithicmonumentsofireland.com

TOORMORE MEGALITHIC TOMB (18)

This Megalithic Tomb, not marked on the OS map, is located on a gentle east facing slope, south of the village of Ruan and SW of the standing stone at **Ruan Commons**. The tomb, orientated NW - SW, consists of two erect orthostats, 0.80m in height, one prostrate stone at SW measuring 1.1m in length, a displaced roofstone, now leaning against one of the erect orthostats and some remains of outer walling at SE. There are some remains of mound/cairn at NW side.

CO-ORDINATES
52 55' 33.961"N...8 59' 51.948"W

POCKET GUIDE SERIES

TOORMORE MEGALITHIC TOMB

www.megalithicmonumentsofireland.com

POCKET GUIDE SERIES

www.megalithicmonumentsofireland.com

STONE ROWS & STONE PAIRS

STONE ROWS

Stone Rows or Stone Alignments are a row of three or more standing stones purposely set upright in the ground in a line and are considered to be aligned to solar and lunar events. The Cork/Kerry group which can consist of up to six standing stones usually 2m in height and positioned on the long axis set in a line and the mid-Ulster group which usually consist of numerous stones, usually not taller than 1m and are often found in association with stone circles and cairns.

STONE PAIRS

Stone Pairs are a sub-group of stone rows and are usually 2m in height and positioned on the long axis in a line. They are considered to have been aligned to various solar and lunar events and some are thought have an association with fertility rites with the stones often been referred to as a male/female pairing.

KNOCKANOURA STONE ROW (19)

Located SE of the school at Clooney, County Clare on a high ridge, stands this Stone Row consisting of three stones. They are marked on the OS maps as **'Knocknafearbreaga Stones'**, which means 'The False Men' in Gaelic, and they get this name from the tale of the monk who was building a church in Tulla and heard the roar of his prized bull being attacked by 3 thieves. He knelt down and prayed, cursing the person who was hurting his bull. The thieves were struck down and became **'farbreags'** or sham-men. The stone row itself consists of three stones, tri-angular in shape and span about 4.2m, with an alignment NE - SW. The 1st stone (NE) measures 1.3m in height, 1.5m in width and 0.35m in depth. The middle stone measures 1.3m in height, 0.70m in width and 0.45m in depth. The 3rd stone (SW) measures 1.5m in height, 1.3m in width and 0.45m in depth.

CO-ORDINATES
52 52' 11.328"N...8 51' 37.57"W

POCKET GUIDE SERIES

KNOCKANOURA STONE ROW

www.megalithicmonumentsofireland.com

TUAMGRANEY STONE PAIR (20)

This Stone Pair, not marked on the OS map, are located north of the Croaghrum River, west of the town of Tuamgraney and 200m NE of a standing stone at **Callaghy**. The pair, aligned E - W, are now sited either side of a field boundary fence, in thick bushes. The east stone, the tallest, is a tri-angular pillar measuring 1.8m in height, 0.55m in width and 0.40m in depth. The west stone is a round boulder, measuring 1.1m in height.

CO-ORDINATES
52 53' 48.02"N...8 32' 41.509"W

www.megalithicmonumentsofireland.com

POCKET GUIDE SERIES

TUAMGRANEY STONE PAIR

POCKET GUIDE SERIES

www.megalithicmonumentsofireland.com

STANDING STONES

A single Standing Stone, or **Gallaun** in Gaelic, is a stone purposely set upright in the ground, usually with an orientation of north-east or south-west but other orientations do occur, and can very in height from 0.50m to 6m but are normally 1.6m high. In the south-west of the island in counties Cork and Kerry, there does seem to be an exception to this, where most standing stones are of a huge size, frequently reaching 4m in height. It is believed they functioned as pre-historic burial markers, commemorative monuments, indicators of ancient route ways or geographical boundaries separating tribal - communal lands. Some standing stones that have been excavated have reveled cremated human remains and pottery shards that date from the Beaker people of the early Bronze Age.

AYLEACOTTY I STANDING STONE (21)

This Standing Stone, along with another stone, both of which are not Marked on the OS map, is located east of the Ardsollus River, **'Abhainn Ath Solas'**, on a gentle, west facing slope. It is a rectangular pillar measuring 1.5m in height, 0.70m in width and 0.40m in depth, with a NE - SW alignment.

CO-ORDINATES
52 47' 37.656"N...8 53' 13.364"W

POCKET GUIDE SERIES

AYLEACOTTY I STANDING STONE

www.megalithicmonumentsofireland.com

AYLEACOTTY II STANDING STONE (22)

This Standing Stone, along with another stone, both of which are not Marked on the OS map, is located east of the Ardsollus River, **'Abhainn Ath Solas'**, on a gentle, west facing slope. It is a round boulder measuring 1.2m in height, 1.2m in width and 0.60m in depth, with a E - W alignment. Close by is a large natural erratic, that may have formed a stone pair.

CO-ORDINATES
52 47' 37.656"N...8 53' 13.364"W

POCKET GUIDE SERIES

AYLEACOTTY II STANDING STONE

www.megalithicmonumentsofireland.com

BALLYROE STANDING STONE (23)

This small Standing Stone, not marked on the OS map, is located west of the Gourna River, 20m from a small road. The stone, aligned NW - SE, measures 1.2m in height, 0.45m in width and 0.25m in depth.

CO-ORDINATES
52 44' 42.15"N...8 44' 36.384"W

POCKET GUIDE SERIES

BALLYROE STANDING STONE

BALLYSHEEN BEG STANDING STONES (24)

These four Standing Stones, marked on the OS map as **'Stones'**, are located in the grounds of Walton Lodge Golf Course along with a megalithic tomb. They range in height from 2.8m - 1.2m and were confirmed as genuine after an archaeological survey in the 1960's.

CO-ORDINATES
52 45' 36.331"N...8 47' 35.871"W

www.megalithicmonumentsofireland.com

POCKET GUIDE SERIES

BALLYSHEEN BEG STANDING STONES

POCKET GUIDE SERIES

CAHERCALLA STANDING STONES (25)

These three Standing Stones, not marked on the Os map, are located west of the Boolyree River, **'Abhlainn Fhraoigh'**, and south of the **'Mound of Magh Adhair'**. They are sited on the edge of a small flood plain and range in height from 1.8m - 1.2m. They have a general alignment of E - W but are not classified as a stone row.

CO-ORDINATES
52 50' 17.247"N...8 50' 17.153"W

POCKET GUIDE SERIES

CAHERCALLA STANDING STONES

69

www.megalithicmonumentsofireland.com

CALLAGHY STANDING STONE (26)

This large monolith, marked on the OS map as **'Stone'**, is located north of the Croaghrum River, west of the town of Tuamgraney and 200m SW of a stone pair at **Tuamgraney**. The stone, split in two vertically, is sited in a garden fence next to the road and measures 2.2m in height, 1.2m in width and 0.80m in depth at the base, with a NE - SW alignment.

CO-ORDINATES
52 53' 46.847"N...8 32' 49.845"W

POCKET GUIDE SERIES

CALLAGHY STANDING STONE

71

www.megalithicmonumentsofireland.com

DEERPARK NORTH I STANDING STONE (27)

This large monolith, not marked on the OS map, is located on the summit of a small hill, west of Lough Cullaunyheeda, **'Loch Choileain Ui Shioda'**, north of the **Craggaunowen Project** and east of the wedge tomb at **Deerpark**. This huge stone, orientated E - W, measures 2.5m in height, 2.1m in width and 1.3m in depth and is composed of sandstone.

CO-ORDINATES
52 48' 57.801"N...8 47' 22.074"W

POCKET GUIDE SERIES

DEERPARK NORTH I STANDING STONE

73

www.megalithicmonumentsofireland.com

POCKET GUIDE SERIES

DEERPARK NORTH II STANDING STONE (28)

This Standing Stone, not marked on the OS map, is located SW of the **Craggaunowen Project**, on the summit of a small hill. The pillar stone, orientated NE - SW, measures 1.8m in height, 0.30m in width and 0.25m in depth and is composed of mudstone.

CO-ORDINATES
52 48' 35.723"N...8 47' 22.248"W

POCKET GUIDE SERIES

DEERPARK NORTH II STANDING STONE

www.megalithicmonumentsofireland.com

KILKIERNAN STANDING STONE (29)

This Standing Stone, not marked on the OS map, is located east of the Ardsollus River, **'Abhainn Ath Solas'**, in the flood plain of that river and west of the standing stones at **Ayleacotty**. The stone, orientated NE - SW and rectangular in plan, measures 1.8m in height, 0.60m in width and 0.60m in depth and is leaning slightly SW.

CO-ORDINATES
52 47' 46.63"N...8 53' 19.445"W

POCKET GUIDE SERIES

KILKIERNAN STANDING STONE

77

www.megalithicmonumentsofireland.com

KNAPPOGUE STANDING STONES (30)

These four Standing Stones, marked on the OS map as **'Pillar Stones'**, are located west of the wedge tomb at **Knopoge**, in the grounds of Knappogue Castle and east of Newmarket-on-Fergus. The stones, rectangular in shape are composed of mudstone and have suffered badly from the effects of weathering. They are 2.1m - 1.8m in height, 1.1m - 0.50m in width and 0.45m - 0.30m in depth with a general NE - SW alignment.

CO-ORDINATES
52 47' 44.041"N...8 49' 42.177"W

POCKET GUIDE SERIES

KNAPPOGUE STANDING STONES

79

www.megalithicmonumentsofireland.com

MOYRIESK STANDING STONE (31)

This large Standing Stone, not marked on the OS map, is located on the summit of a low hill in generally level pasture. The stone, aligned NNE - SSW, measures 2.1m in height, 1.7m in width and 1m in depth and is composed of local limestone.

CO-ORDINATES
52 51' 41.449"N...8 53' 56.928"W

POCKET GUIDE SERIES

MOYRIESK STANDING STONE

RUAN COMMONS STANDING STONE (32)

This Standing Stone, not marked on the OS map, is located on a gentle west facing slope, south of the modern church in Ruan village and NE of the megalithic tomb at **Toormore**. The pillar stone, with a general NE - SW alignment, measures 1.7m in height, 0.30m in width and 0.20m in depth.

CO-ORDINATES
52 55' 38.829"N...8 59' 26.853"W

POCKET GUIDE SERIES

RUAN COMMONS STANDING STONE

83

www.megalithicmonumentsofireland.com

SKEHANAGH STANDING STONE (33)

This large monolith, marked on the OS map as **'Stone'**, is located in the flood plain of the River Fergus, **'An Forghas'**, west of Clarecastle, **'Droichean an Chlair'**, in marshy bog-land. The stone, orientated NE - SW, measures 2.9m in height, 0.90m in width and 0.60m in depth and is leaning heavily SW.

CO-ORDINATES
52 48' 53.071"N...8 57' 19.802"W

POCKET GUIDE SERIES

SKEHANAGH STANDING STONE

85

www.megalithicmonumentsofireland.com

TOONAGH STANDING STONE (34)

This Standing Stone, marked on the OS map as **'Stone'**, is located 150m west of **The Mound of Magh Adhair**, west of the Hell's River. The stone, aligned NE - SW, measures 2m in height, 0.90m in width and 0.20m in depth and is composed of red sandstone. Its alignment indicates that it is probably a Bronze Age monolith and therefore earlier than the Ring-Fort to the east.

CO-ORDINATES
52 50' 27.995"N...8 49' 49.031"W

www.megalithicmonumentsofireland.com

POCKET GUIDE SERIES

TOONAGH STANDING STONE

87

www.megalithicmonumentsofireland.com

TYREDAGH STANDING STONE (35)

This large Standing Stone, marked on the OS map as **'Megalithic Tombs'**, is located on a gentle south facing slope in otherwise level pasture, 100m from a small road. It measures 2.8m in height, 0.80m in width and 0.60m in depth.

CO-ORDINATES
52 53' 16.64"N...8 48' 40.49"W

POCKET GUIDE SERIES

TYREDAGH STANDING STONE

89

www.megalithicmonumentsofireland.com

POCKET GUIDE SERIES

www.megalithicmonumentsofireland.com

OGHAM STONES

Ogham stones can be upright monoliths or recumbent slabs, onto which ogham script has been incised. Ogham script consists of groups of 1-5 parallel lines and notches cut along the side or across the edge of a stone to represent the sounds of the Irish language. It is usually read up the left angle. The inscription gives a person's name (usually male) and immediate decedent/s or tribal ancestor. The stones may have functioned as memorials, grave markers or territorial markers and date from the late 4th to the early 8th century AD.

SHANTRAUD OGHAM-RUNIC STONE (36)

This is a very rare and historical stone, for it has inscriptions in both Ogham and Runic and can be found in the Cathedral in Killaloe, County Clare. It is the only known example in the world of a bi-lingual stone with inscription in both the Irish Ogham and Scandinavian Runic. Both inscriptions refer to the same person so it can be assumed that this person was an actual historical figure. The ogham inscription reads as "BEANDACHT (AR) - TOROQR (IM)", this translates as **'a blessing upon Thorgrim'** while the runic reads as "URGRIM RISTI KRUS INA" which translates as **'Thorgrim carved this stone'**. It is 0.89m in height, 0.46m in width, 0.20m in depth and has been dated by Ziegler to 899 - 1199 AD.

CO-ORDINATES
52 48' 22.32"N...8 26' 21.312"W

POCKET GUIDE SERIES

SHANTRAUD OGHAM RUNIC STONE

93

www.megalithicmonumentsofireland.com

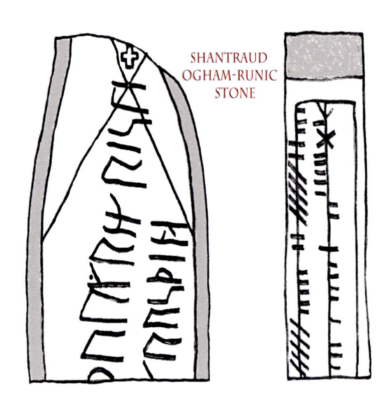

SHANTRAUD OGHAM & RUNIC SCORES

BULLAUN STONES

The term 'bullaun' from the Irish word **'bullán'**, which means a round hollow in a stone, or a bowl is applied to boulders of stone or bedrock with hemispherical hollows or basin-like depressions, which may have functioned as mortars. They are frequently associated with ecclesiastical sites and Holy Wells and so may have been used for religious purposes. Other examples which do not appear to have ecclesiastical associations can be found in bedrock or outcrop in upland contexts, often under blanket bog, and are known as bedrock mortars. They date from the prehistoric period to the early medieval period, 5th - 12th centuries AD.

FINLOUGH BULLAUN STONE (37)

This Bullaun Stone, marked on the OS map as **'Altar'**, is located in front of a holy shrine in the grounds of a graveyard, on the north shore of Finn Lough, **'Fionn Loch', and** west of the wedge tomb at **Fenloe**. The circular bullaun is now embedded into a concrete wall capping and measures 0.35m in diameter and 0.30m in depth.

CO-ORDINATES
52 46' 53.325"N...8 50' 14.294"W

www.megalithicmonumentsofireland.com

POCKET GUIDE SERIES

FINLOUGH BULLAUN STONE

www.megalithicmonumentsofireland.com

POCKET GUIDE SERIES

www.megalithicmonumentsofireland.com

POCKET GUIDE SERIES

OTHER SITES

These are some other monuments in the county that are of historical interest. They can include a wide variety of monuments from Neolithic cairns and rock art, Iron Age Hill-Forts and Stone-Forts to Anglo-Norman Castles, Mottes, Museums and Monasteries.

www.megalithicmonumentsofireland.com

CAHERCONNELL STONE FORT (38)

The Stone Fort, **'Caher'**, at Caherconnell, marked on the OS map as **'Caherlisnanroum'**, is one of the many ring forts to be found in Ireland and is one of the finest examples to be found in County Clare. It's an almost perfect circular shape, 40m in diameter, which is twice the diameter of the average stone fort. The walls are up to 4m in width and in some places 3m in height. Ring forts like this, were in use from 400 to 1,200 AD, but there is evidence to suggest Caherconnell may have been occupied up until the 14th - 15th centuries. Archaeological excavations have taken place at the site in 2007, '08 and '09. The 2008 dig was centered around a prehistoric chamber, originally thought to have been a souterrain, 30m south east of the fort. The 2008 excavation however, revealed a dry-stone circular chamber with a short passage at the north-east. Artefacts found in the chamber, such as chert , flint flakes, tools, two pieces of prehistoric pottery and a broken polished stone axe, are associated with the Early Bronze Age in Ireland, 2,000-1,500 BC. Found within the passage to the chamber, were two burials of human remains, which were radio carbon dated to 1430-1530 AD and 1560-1630 AD. Interestingly one of the human remains was disarticulated, a ritual normally found in much earlier times, 3,700 BC. There is now a visitor center close by, with an excellent audio-visual exhibit.

POCKET GUIDE SERIES

CAHERCONNELL STONE FORT

101

www.megalithicmonumentsofireland.com

POCKET GUIDE SERIES

THE MOUND OF MAGH ADHAIR ROYAL INAUGURATION SITE (39)

Magh Adhair is a well preserved place of ancient ritual and ceremonial inauguration, where a long succession of the Kings of Thomond (O'Brien) were inaugurated here down to the reign of Queen Elizabeth I. The mound is situated in Toonagh between the parishes of Clooney and Tulla and stands in a small plain, in a natural amphitheatre, formed by a low crag called 'the Beetle's Crag' or **'Cragnakeeroge'**, beside the 'Hell Bridge' and 'Hell River'. There are traces of a semi-circular ditch, and between which lies a large block of conglomerate of dull purple, with red and pink pebbles of porphyry and quartz. The stone has two basins in it and it is said that the future king would wash his hands before his inauguration on the mound. On the **'dún'**, built by Adhair, one of the Firbolgs, is a tree which was known locally as the **'Bille'**. Under this tree the kings of Thomond used to be crowned, up until the 12th - 13th centuries, the most famous of these was Brian Ború, **'Bóruma mac Cennétig'**, (941–23 April 1014) the High King of Ireland, killed at the Battle of Clontarf, **'Cath Chluain Tarbh'**, in 1014 AD.

CO-ORDINATES
52 50' 27.995"N...8 49' 49.031"W

POCKET GUIDE SERIES

MOUND OF MAGH ADHAIR

103

www.megalithicmonumentsofireland.com

THE CRAGGAUNOWEN PROJECT (40)

The Craggaunowen Project is where Celtic life is brought to life. The prize-winning visitor centre is dedicated to interpreting Ireland's Pre-historic and early Christian eras and it's exhibits range from Bronze-Age homesteads to Celtic Chieftain's residences. The Project is also known as **'Craggaunowen: The Living Past'** and was founded by noted archaeologist, John Hunt in 1960. Hunt was also a historian, antiquarian and collector and upon his death, his collections were donated to the city of Limerick and are now housed in the Hunt Museum, originally the Customs House. It was also Hunt who encouraged Lord Gort to restore the now world famous Bunratty Castle. Getting his inspiration from his excavations along the shores of Lough Derg, Hunt established this open-air museum on the estate at Craggaunowen Castle, built by John MacSioda MacNamara in 1550 and now contains display pieces from some of Hunt's excavations.

CO-ORDINATES
52 48' 37.134"N...8 47' 51.024"W

www.megalithicmonumentsofireland.com

POCKET GUIDE SERIES

THE CRAGGAUNOWEN PROJECT

www.megalithicmonumentsofireland.com

GLOSSARY

THE THREE AGE- SYSTEM

In Denmark in the mid 1800's, two men, Christian Thomsen and Jens Worsaae, developed a system of classification of prehistory called The Three Age system. They concluded that prehistory can be divided into three ages - The Stone Age, the Bronze Age and the Iron Age, with the Stone Age being sub divided into the Paleolithic, Mesolithic and Neolithic periods. They stated that effective classification was indispensable to the advance of the study of prehistory, and The Three Age system - with sub divisions - remains a fundamental framework for understanding prehistory in much of the world.

A…An Alignment (or Stone Row) is a linear arrangement of upright, parallel megalithic standing stones set at intervals along a common axis or series of axes, usually dating from the late Neolithic to the Bronze Age.

B… Barrow is a mound of earth and stones raised over a grave or graves. A barrow composed largely or entirely of stones is usually referred to as a cairn. They are also known as Tumulus, burial mounds, Hugelgrab or Kurgans.

A Boulder Burial is a large boulder or capstone of megalithic proportions, resting on a number of supporting stones, usually 3 or 4 in number, which, in most cases, do not form a recognizable chamber structure. Excavations a Bronze Age date for this burial monument, 2,400-500 BC.

The Bronze Age 2,500 BC-700 BC, is the 2nd principal period in the three-age system for classifying prehistoric societies, preceded by the Stone Age. Its date and context vary depending on the country or geographical region.

A Bullaun is a term used for the depression in a stone. The size of the bullaun is variable and these hemispherical cups hollowed out of a rock may come as singles or multiples with the same rock.

C… A Cairn is an artificial pile of stones, often in a conical form. They are usually found in uplands, on moorland, on mountaintops or near waterways.

A Capstone is a large, sometimes enormous, stone covering the top of an archaeological tomb.

The **Chalcolithic** period or Copper Age period, is a phase in the development of human culture in which the use of early metal tools appeared alongside the use of stone tools. This period is outside the traditional three-age system and occurs between the Neolithic and Bronze Age around 2,500 BC-2,000 BC.

A **Cist** is a Bronze Age burial set in the ground consisting of a small slab lined box with a single stone slab used as a cover.

A **Court** tomb is generally a long rectangular or trapezoidal cairn, at the broader end of which is usually a U-shaped un-roofed forecourt area.

A **Crannog** is a man-made enclosure, built on a lake and reached via an artificial causeway. They date from the late Bronze Age to the Iron Age.

Cruciform is the shape of the burial chamber which can be found in passage tombs mirroring the shape of the cross.

A **Cup Mark** is a small, man made depression used as a decoration on stones and is hemispherical in shape.

D...A **Dolmen** (also known as cromlech, anta, Hunengrab, Hunebed, quoit and portal dolmen) is a type of single-chamber megalithic tomb, usually consisting of 3 or more upright stones supporting a large flat horizontal capstone. Most date from the early Neolithic period.

E...An **Equinox** in astronomy is the moment in time when the centre of the Sun can be observed to be directly above the Earth's equator, occurring around March 20th and September 23rd each year.

F...A **Four-Poster** stone circle is an arrangement of four upright stones standing at the corners of an irregular quadrilateral. The stones are usually graded in height with the tallest stone at either the south-west or north-east corner. These monuments are closely related to stone circles in date and function though they are much less numerous and only six having been recorded in Ireland. These are dated to the Bronze Age (2,400-500 BC).

G...A **Gallery** is what archaeologists refer to as the burial chamber in wedge tombs and court tombs.

H…A Henge is a circular monument consisting of an outer earthen bank and an inner ditch.
A Hill-fort is a large area, from 3 to 22 hectares, located on and often following the natural contours of a hill, enclosed by an earth or stone bank. They have been dated to the late Bronze Age around 1,000-500 BC.

I…In history, the Iron Age 700 BC-500 AD, is the last principal period in the three-age system for classifying prehistoric societies, preceded by the Bronze Age. Its date and context vary depending on the country or geographical region.

J…Jambs are two stones either side of a burial chamber forming a door way or sub-chamber.

K…A Kerb is a ring of stones set around a cairn or mound, used to retain the cairn or earth in place.

L…A Linkardstown tomb is a circular mound covering a central large cist or chamber which contains an inhumed burial/burials, of usually one or two males, with distinctive decorated pottery. Radiocarbon dates of these burials centre around 3, 500 BC, early Neolithic.

A Lintel is a stone placed flat across a passage to form a roof.

M...A Megalith is a large stone which has been used to construct a structure or monument, either alone or together with other stones. The word Megalith comes from the ancient Greek, **megas** meaning great and **lithos** meaning stone.

Megalithic means structures made of such large stones, utilizing an interlocking system without the use of mortar or cement.

A Menhir is another name for a standing stone. It is a combination of two words from the Breton Language--- Men (stone) and hir (long).

The Mesolithic period (8,000 BC- 4,500 BC) also known as the Middle Stone Age, is what historians refer to as the 2nd of the three periods of the Stone Age. At this time homo-sapiens survived by a nomadic hunter-gatherer lifestyle with no permanent settlements.

A midden is a refuse heap sometimes surviving as a layer or spread. These may be of any date from prehistory (8,000 BC - 400 AD) up to the medieval period (5th - 16th centuries AD).

N…The Neolithic period (4,500 BC-2,500 BC),also known as the New Stone Age, is what historians refer to as the last of the three periods of the Stone age. It is when homo-sapiens began to cultivate the land and give up their hunter-gathering life style. It also marks the period when construction of enormous tombs began.

O…Ogham is sometimes referred to as 'The Celtic Tree-Alphabet'. It was the name given to the scribing of the Old Gaelic language and was used on standing stones. It could also be found later scribed on a few tombs and recumbent stones. It is believed to date from around 400 AD but maybe a lot earlier.

An Orthostat is a large upright stone used to form the walls of megalithic tombs.

An Outlier is a standing stone positioned outside a stone circle usually for a compass point or astronomical alignment.

P…The term Paleolithic refers to a prehistoric era distinguished by the development of the first stone tools. It covers the greatest portion of humanity's time on Earth, extending from 2.5 million years BC to the Mesolithic, 8,000 BC. It is sub-divided into Lower, Middle and Upper Paleolithic.

A **Passage** tomb is a type of tomb where by the burial chamber is reached by way of a long passage from the entrance to the tomb.

Portal stones are a pair of matched upright stones that form the doorway and also support the capstone at the front of a portal tomb. They are usually taller the other uprights.

R…A **Recumbent** stone in the case of a circle, is when the stone is wider than it is taller. When describing a standing stone, it's when the stone has fallen.

Runic was used to write various Germanic languages and their Scandinavian variants. The earliest runic inscriptions date from around 150 AD and were generally replaced by Latin along with Christianization around 700 AD in central Europe and by 1100 AD in Scandinavia. The origins of Runic are uncertain but many characters bear a close resemblance to Latin.

S……**Solstices** occur twice a year, when the tilt of the earth's axis is most oriented toward or away from the Sun, causing the Sun to reach its northern most and southern most extremes. These occur around June 20th (summer solstice) and December 22nd (winter solstice).

A **Souterrain** is an underground structure consisting of one or more chambers, connected by narrow passageways or creep-ways, usually constructed of dry-stone walling with a lintelled roof over the passages and a corbelled roof over the chambers .Most souterrains appear to have been built in the early medieval period as a defensive feature and/or for storage.

The **Stone** Age is a broad prehistoric time period during which humans widely used stone for tool-making. It spans a vast time period, 2.5 million years BC-2,500 BC. As such it is sub-divided into Paleolithic, Mesolithic and Neolithic and these three periods are further sub-divided.

A **Stone Circle** is a circular or oval setting of spaced, upright stones with their broad sides facing inwards, towards the centre. The Cork/Kerry series is characterized by an uneven number orthostats which decrease in height from the entrance stones to the recumbent stone opposite the entrance. The Ulster series is defined by low orthostats which often occur in groups and are associated with long stone rows. Stone circles have their origin in the Neolithic though they are primarily a Bronze Age ritual monument.

W…A **Wedge** tomb can generally be defined as wider and taller at one end and so are wedge shaped in plan and profile.

POCKET GUIDE SERIES

INDEX OF IMAGES

Poulnabrone Portal Tomb……………..*Front cover*
1. Map of County Clare…………………..*page…12*
2. Clogher Portal Tomb……………………*page…17*
3. Moyree Commons Portal Tomb…………*page…19*
4. Poulnabrone Portal Tomb………………*page…21*
5. Ballinphunta Wedge Tomb………………*page…23*
6. Ballyganner South Wedge Tomb………..*page…25*
7. Deerpark North Wedge Tomb…………..*page…27*
8. Fenloe Wedge Tomb……………………*page…29*
9. Gleninsheen Wedge Tomb………………*page…31*
10. Kilvoydan North Wedge Tomb…………*page…33*
11. Knocknalappa Wedge Tomb……………*page…35*
12. Knopoge Wedge Tomb…………………*page…37*
13. Meggagh Wedge Tomb…………………*page…39*
14. Milltown Wedge Tomb…………………*page…41*
15. Newgrove Wedge Tomb…………………*page…43*
16. Parknabinna Wedge Tomb………………*page…45*
17. Ballysheen Beg Megalithic Tomb………*page…47*
18. Deerpark Megalithic Tomb………………*page…49*
19. Toormore Megalithic Tomb………………*page…51*

www.megalithicmonumentsofireland.com

20. Knockanoura Stone Row……….……..…*page…55*
21. Tuamgraney Stone Pair………………….*page…57*
22. Ayleacotty I Standing Stone…………….*page…61*
23. Ayleacotty II Standing Stone…………...*page…63*
24. Ballyroe Standing Stone…………………*page…65*
25. Ballysheen Beg Standing Stones……....*page…67*
26. Cahercalla Standing Stones…………….*page…69*
27. Callaghy Standing Stone…………..……*page…71*
28. Deerpark North I Standing Stone………*page…73*
29. Deerpark North II Standing Stone…....…*page…75*
30. Kilkiernan Standing Stone………………*page…77*
31. Knappogue Standing Stones……………*page…79*
32. Moyriesk Standing Stone……………….*page…81*
33. Ruan Commons Standing Stone……....*page…83*
34. Skehanagh Standing Stone…………….*page…85*
35. Toonagh Standing Stone…………….…*page…87*
36. Tyredagh Standing Stone……………...*page…89*
37. Shantraud Ogham-Runic Stone………..*page…93*
38. Drawing of Shantraud Stone…………..*page…94*
39. Fenlough Bullaun Stone…………….…*page…97*
40. Caherconnell Stone Fort…….…………*page..101*
41. The Mound of Magh Adhair……………*page..103*
42. The Craggaunowen Project…………..*page..105*

ALL IMAGES © by AUTHOR
(Except Magh Adhair © Megalithic Portal)

SPECIAL NOTES

VISITING MONUMENTS

The majority of these monuments, as with 90% of all national monuments on the island, are on privately owned land. When visiting any of these monuments, please seek permission from the land owners if required. Please do not litter or disturb the monuments.

MAPS

The maps shown in this book are for illustrative purposes only and should be viewed as such. For more detailed maps, consult the official O S I maps for the county.

CO-ORDINATES

The co-ordinates given for each monument are accurate to within 10m and are based on GPS co-ordinates.

www.megalithicmonumentsofireland.com

POCKET GUIDE SERIES

www.megalithicmonumentsofireland.com

POCKET GUIDE SERIES

www.megalithicmonumentsofireland.com

POCKET GUIDE SERIES

www.megalithicmonumentsofireland.com

Made in the USA
Columbia, SC
15 March 2023